PIANO SOLO

CONTEMPORARY WORSHIP CLASSICS

10 RICHLY ARRANGED PIANO SOLOS

By Mark Hayes

T0083373

ISBN 978-1-70515-475-5

HAL•LEONARD®

Visit Hal Leonard Online at
www.halleonard.com

World headquarters, contact:
Hal Leonard
7777 West Bluemound Road
Milwaukee, WI 53213
Email: info@halleonard.com

In Europe, contact:
Hal Leonard Europe Limited
1 Red Place
London, W1K 6PL
Email: info@halleonardeurope.com

In Australia, contact:
Hal Leonard Australia Pty. Ltd.
4 Lentara Court
Cheltenham, Victoria, 3192 Australia
Email: info@halleonard.com.au

ABOUT THE ARRANGER

MARK HAYES is an award-winning concert pianist, composer, arranger and conductor of international renown. His personal catalog totals over 1,500 published works of all kinds. Mark received a Bachelor of Music degree (summa cum laude) in Piano Performance from Baylor University in 1975. He has conducted the SWACDA & MCDA Community & Church Honor Choir and has served as a frequent guest conductor at Lincoln Center, the National Cathedral and Carnegie Hall, featuring works such as his *Te Deum, Magnificat, Gloria* and *International Carol Suites*.

In 2010, Baylor University Center for Christian Music Studies honored Mark with the Award for Exemplary Leadership in Christian Music. He conducted the world premiere of his *Requiem* at Lincoln Center in May 2013. In October 2014, Hayes conducted his *Requiem* at St. Ignatius Basilica in Rome, Italy as part of The Festival Pro Musica E Arte Sacra, sponsored by the Vatican. He was commissioned by St. Paul's Co-educational College in Hong Kong to write a work for treble voices, mixed voices and orchestra for their 100th anniversary and also conducted the world premiere in Hong Kong (December 2015).

Hayes wrote the musical score for *Civil War Voices*, which won six awards at the Midtown International Theatre Festival in New York City (July 2010). He orchestrated the hit musical *Madame Buttermilk* by Ross Carter and arranged the music for *We'll Meet Again*, a new musical by Jim Harris.

Mark's passion is writing for the piano. He has over 100 piano books in print, spanning a variety of styles such as Gospel, Classical, Jazz and Broadway. In addition to his involvement in the sacred and secular choral music fields, Hayes is an accomplished orchestrator and record producer. Whether concertizing on the other side of the globe or composing at his home in Kansas City, Missouri, Mark is blessed to live out his mission "to create beautiful music for the world."

PREFACE

The contemporary worship scene has a rich canon of songs from which to choose that includes songs from the 1970s to the current day. The talented keyboard editorial team at Hal Leonard chose ten of the most widely sung worship songs of the last decade and invited me to arrange them in my unique style. If you have played my piano solos, you know that I enjoy finding rich chord substitutions and interesting harmonic progressions. My improvisatory style draws from the light jazz tradition as well as contemporary pop music.

The worship songs in this collection were written in the simple, straightforward harmonic language that is especially useful for songwriters who are primarily guitarists. While being mindful that the power of these songs is often in their simplicity, I offer a rich, new way of expressing them in worship. I have re-imagined some of the chord progressions, introduced lush harmonies in places, and added contemporary embellishments and interludes.

You'll notice there are chord labels throughout this book. I find that to be a helpful learning tool. When I was first exposed to jazz harmonies, I wondered how in the world I could replicate them when I improvised. Seeing the chord label and the notes spelled out on the page was the first step in understanding them and being able to use them in my improvisation and arranging. Whether you play by ear or only read music, I hope this additional information will help you expand your harmonic vocabulary and improvisatory skills.

Mark Hayes

AMAZING GRACE
(My Chains Are Gone)

Words by JOHN NEWTON
Traditional American Melody
Additional Words and Music by CHRIS TOMLIN
and LOUIE GIGLIO
Arranged by Mark Hayes

Slowly

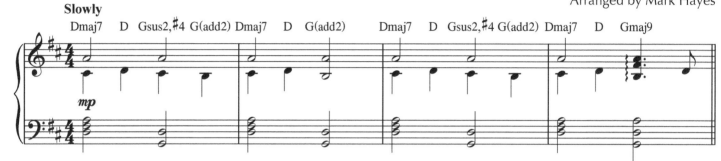

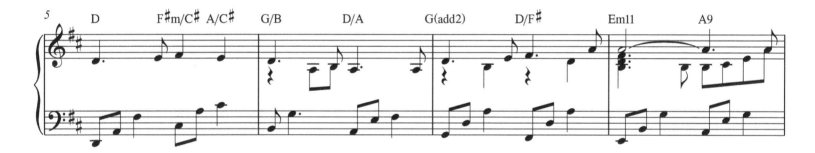

Duration: 2:50

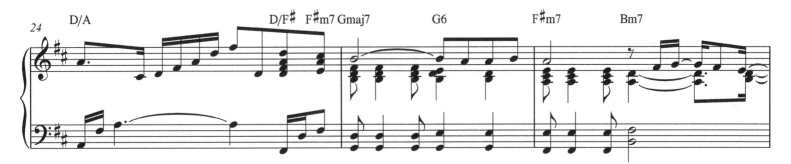

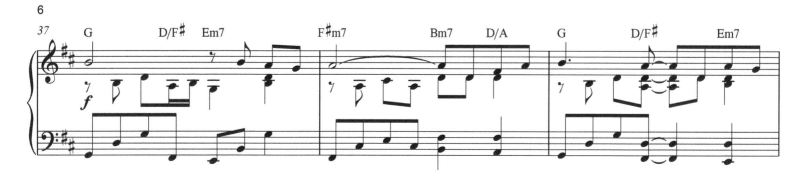

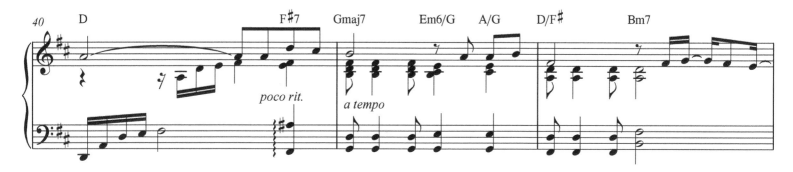

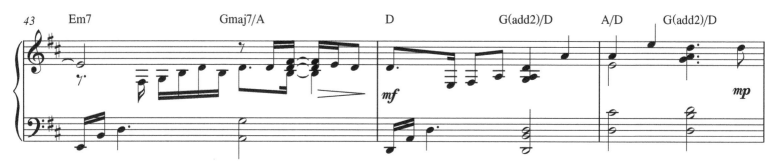

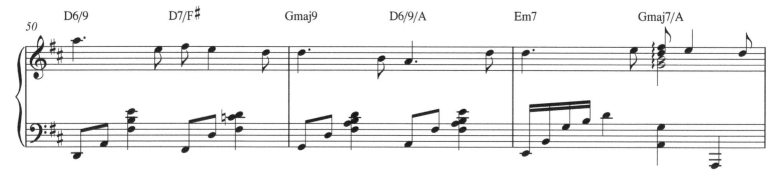

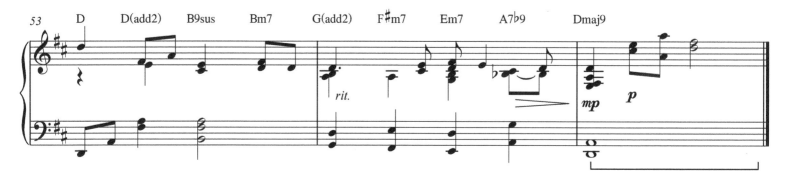

HOW DEEP THE FATHER'S LOVE FOR US

Words and Music by
STUART TOWNEND
Arranged by Mark Hayes

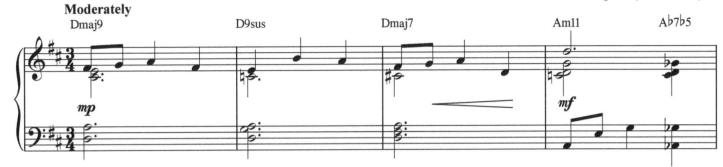

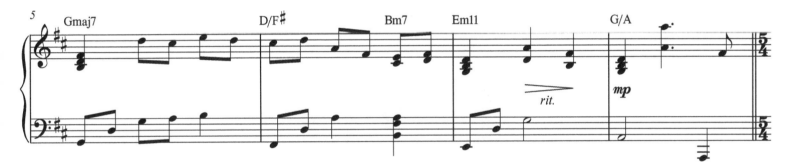

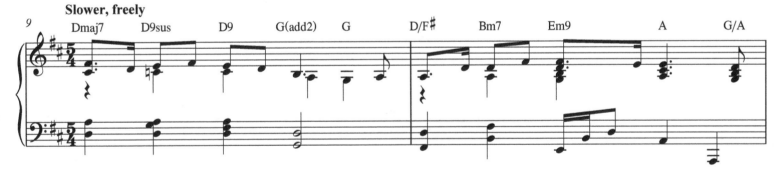

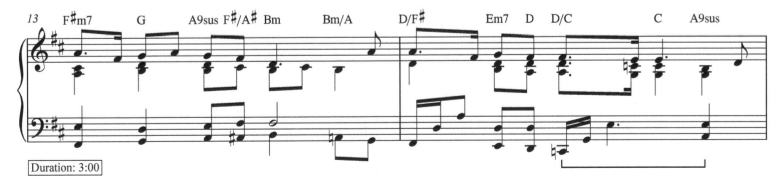

Duration: 3:00

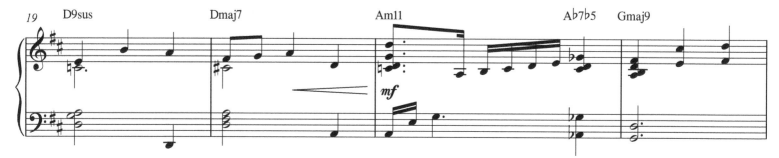

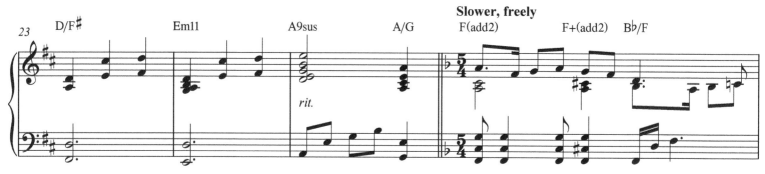

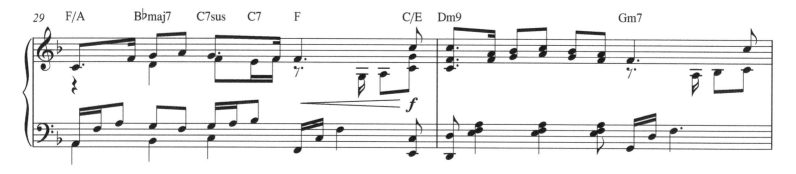

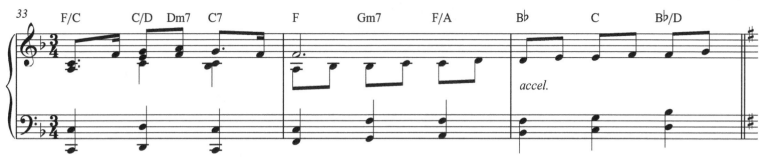

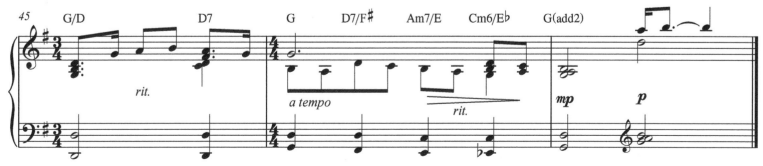

CORNERSTONE

Words and Music by JONAS MYRIN,
REUBEN MORGAN, ERIC LILJERO
and EDWARD MOTE
Arranged by Mark Hayes

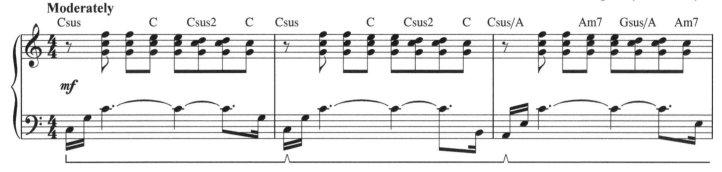

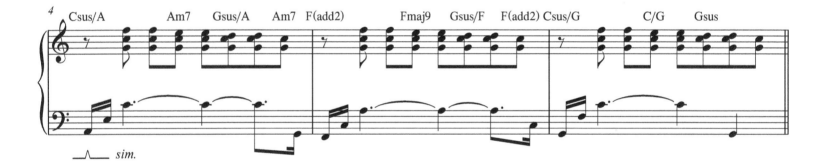

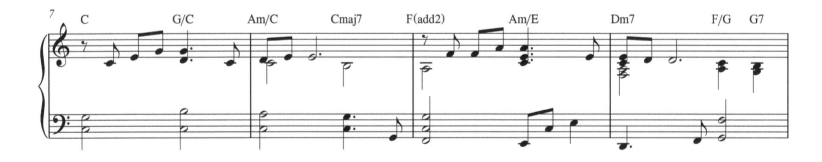

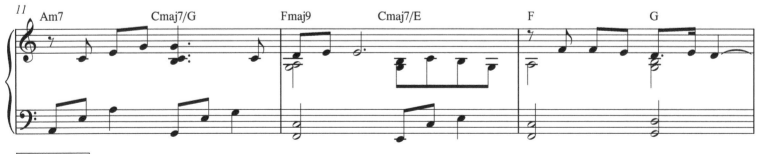

Duration: 3:05

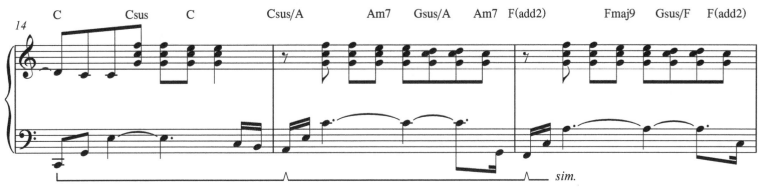

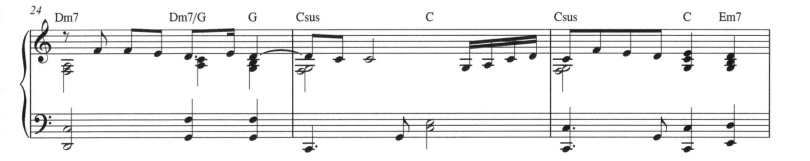

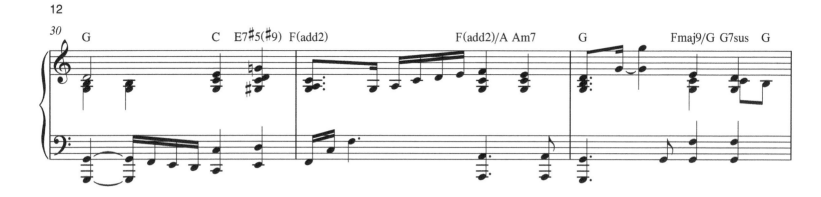

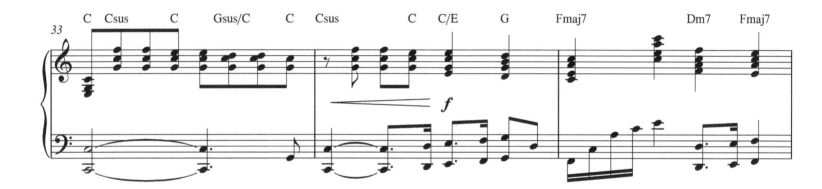

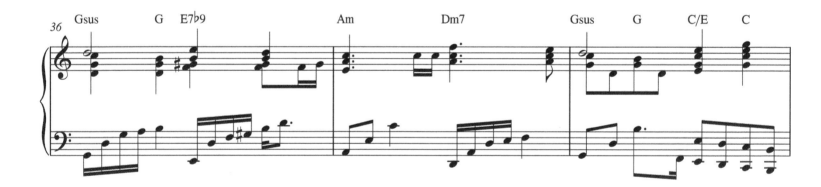

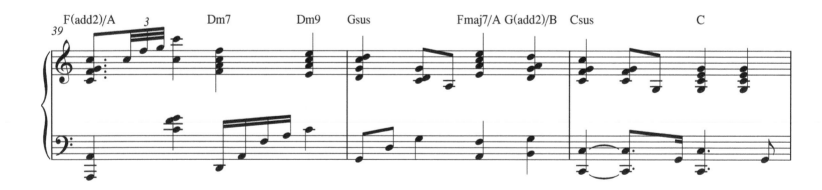

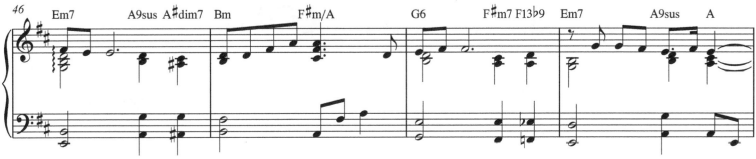

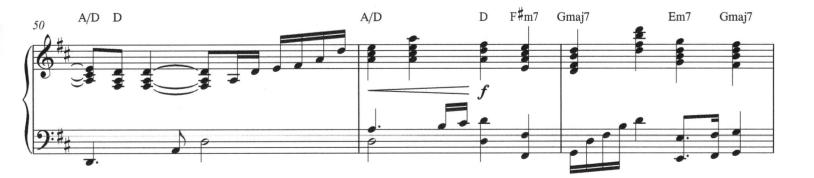

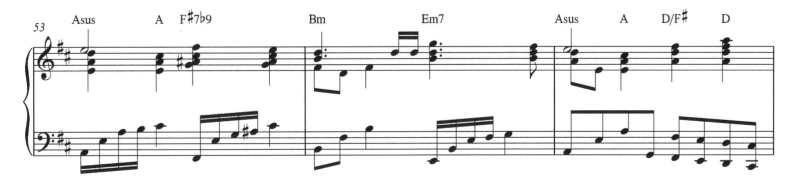

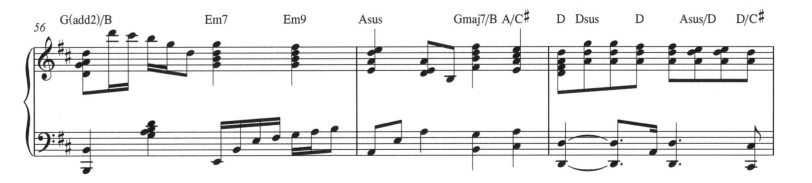

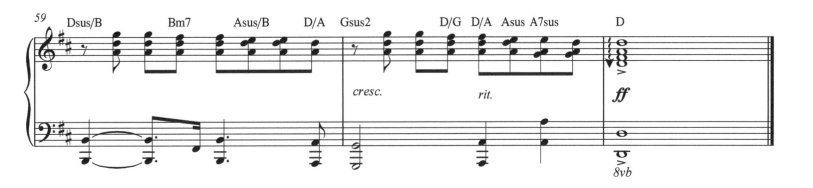

IN CHRIST ALONE

Words and Music by KEITH GETTY
and STUART TOWNEND
Arranged by Mark Hayes

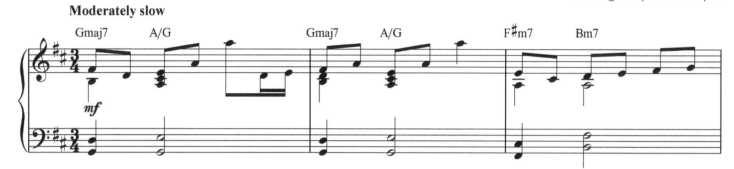

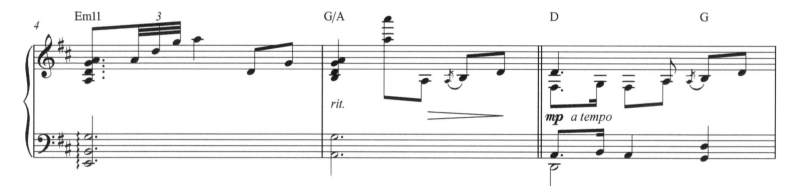

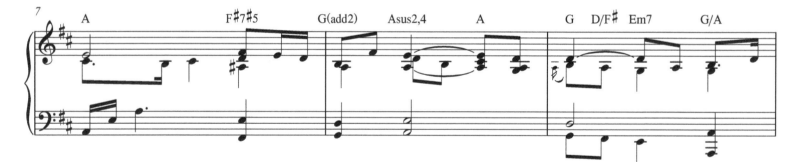

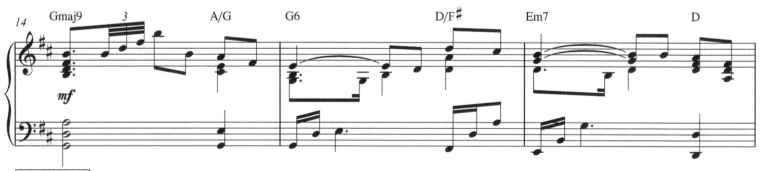

Duration: 2:45

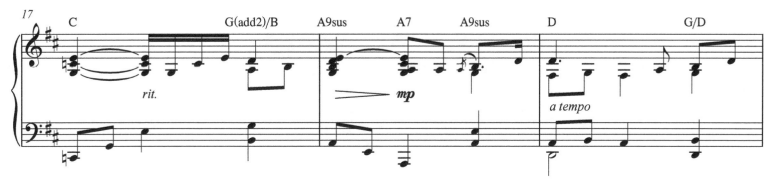

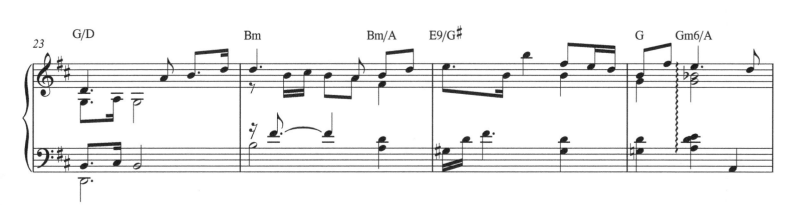

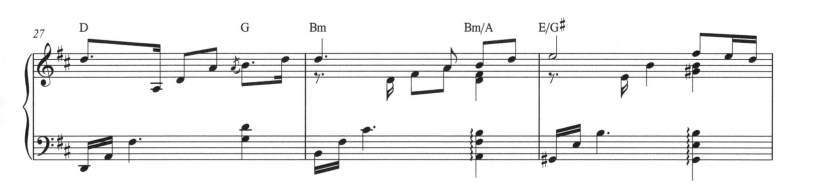

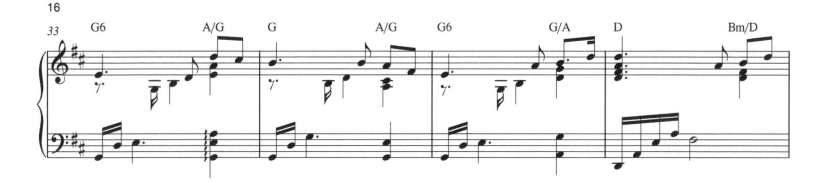

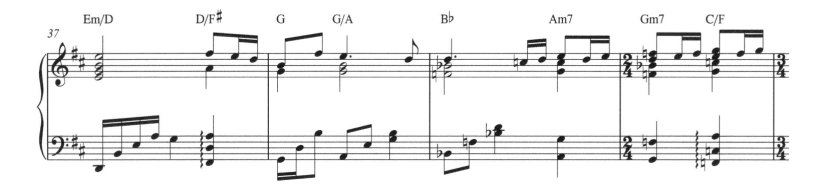

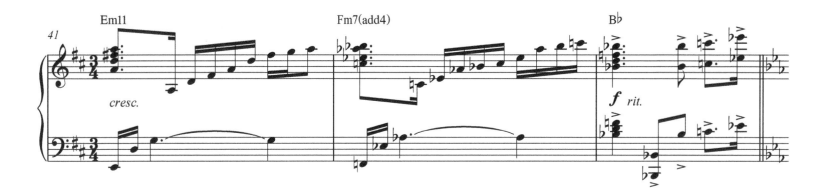

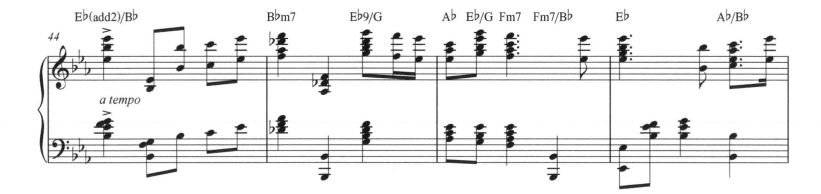

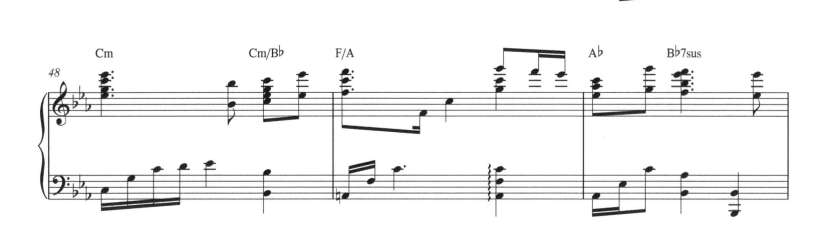

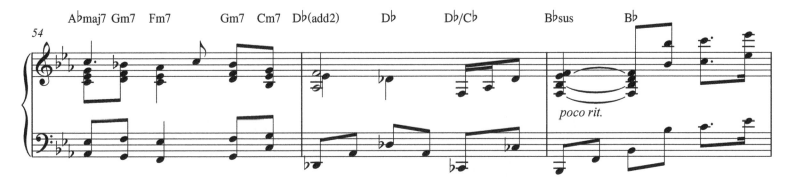

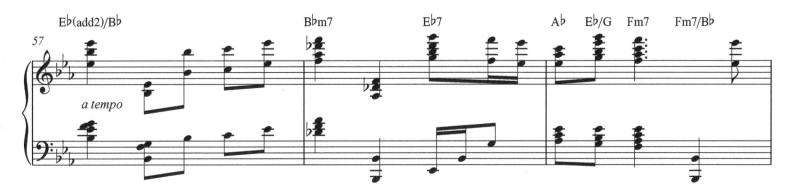

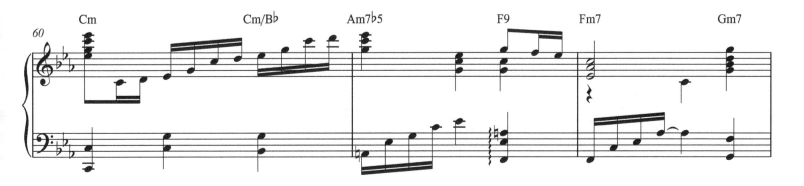

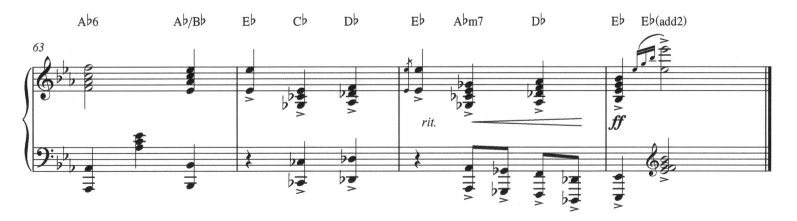

LIVING HOPE

Words and Music by PHIL WICKHAM
and BRIAN JOHNSON
Arranged by Mark Hayes

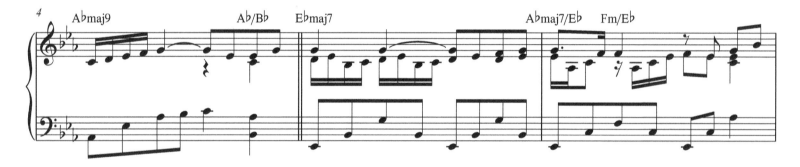

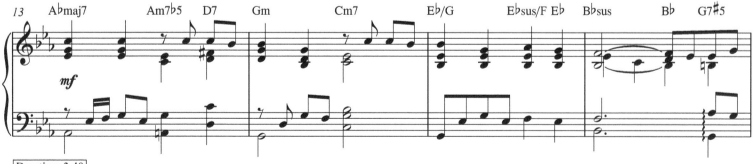

Duration: 3:40

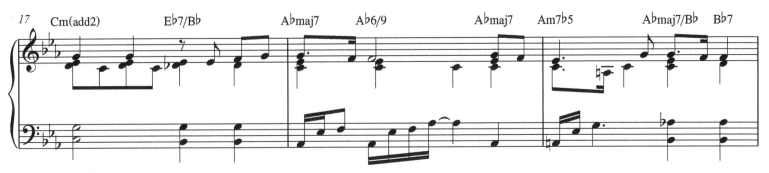

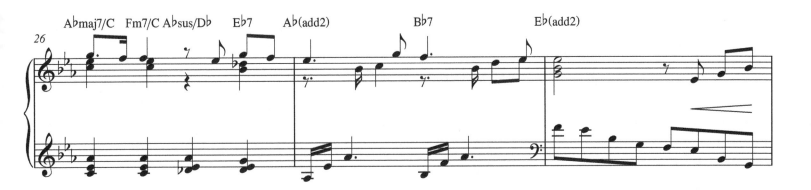

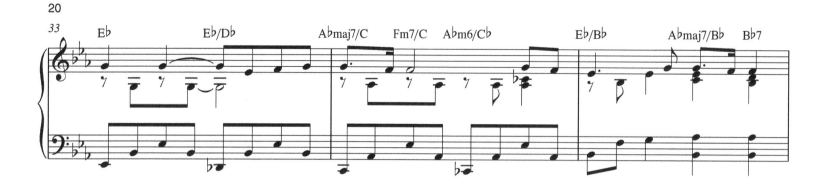

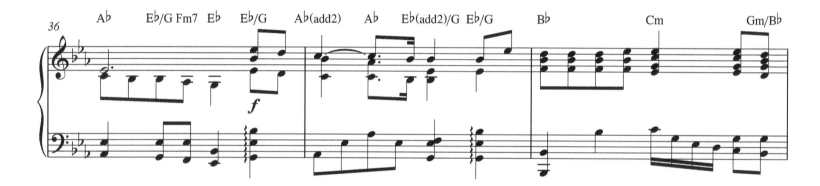

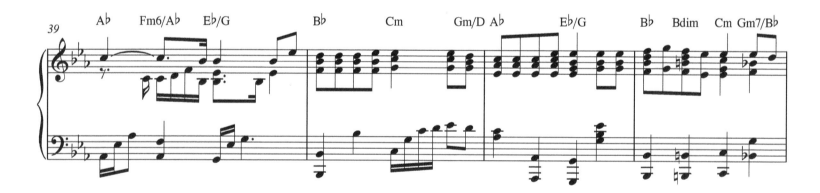

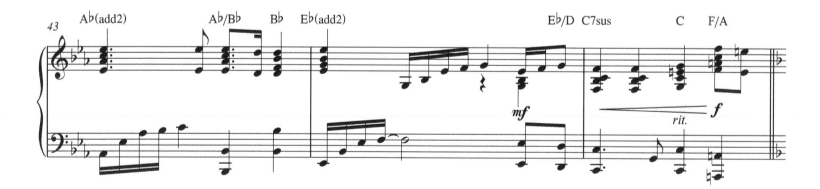

Broadly, somewhat slower

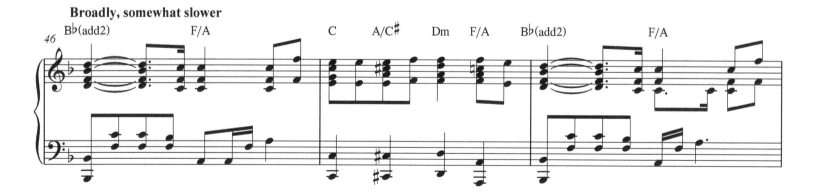

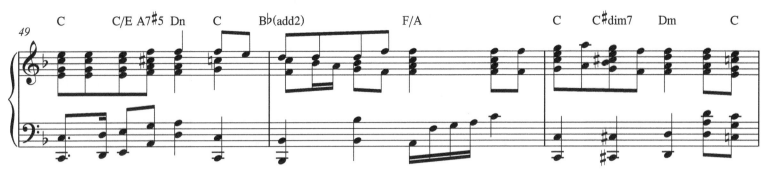

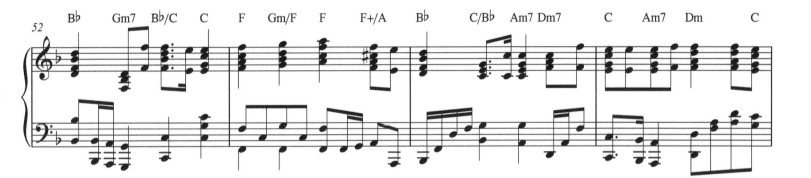

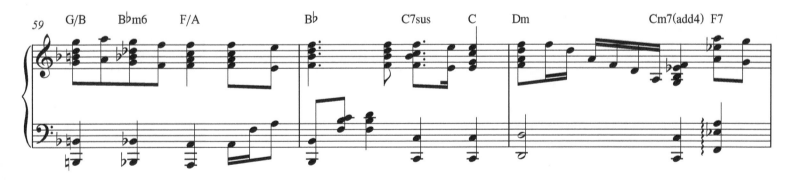

LORD, I NEED YOU

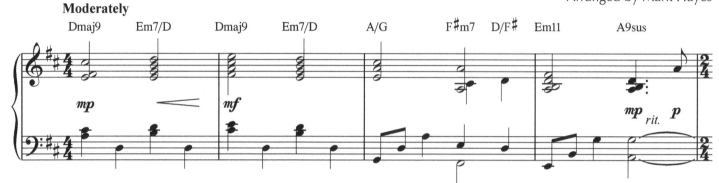

Words and Music by JESSE REEVES,
KRISTIAN STANFILL, MATT MAHER,
CHRISTY NOCKELS and DANIEL CARSON
Arranged by Mark Hayes

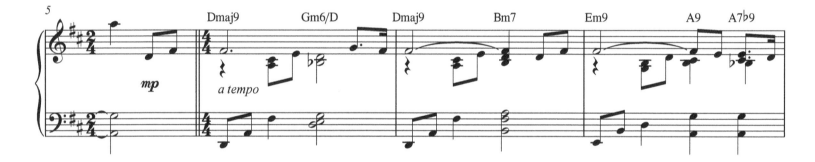

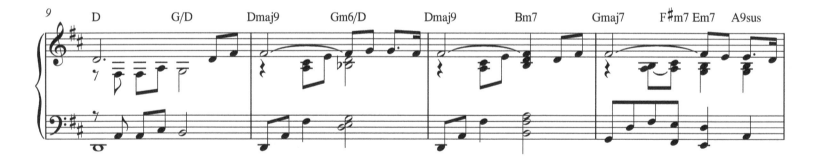

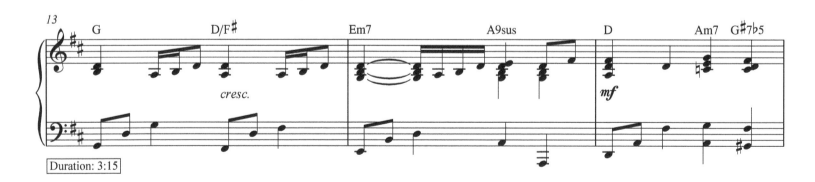

Duration: 3:15

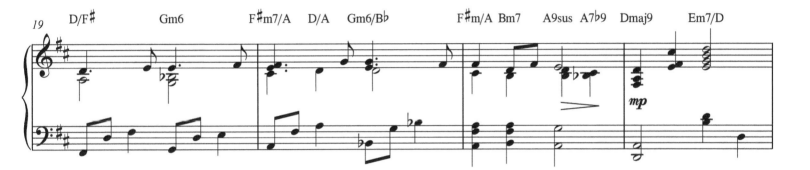
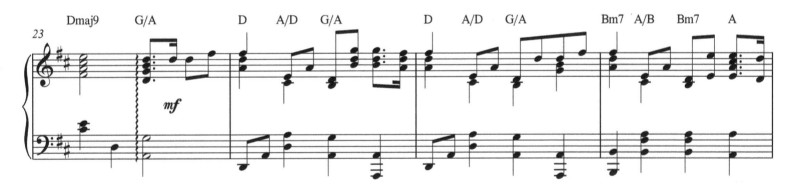
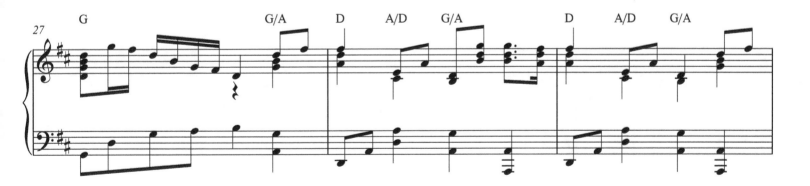

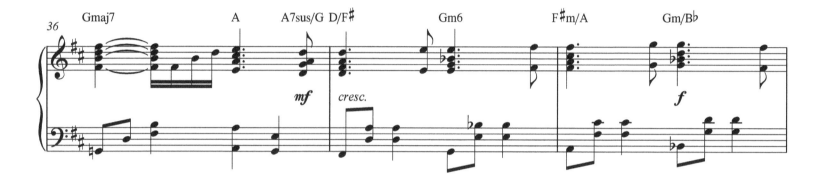

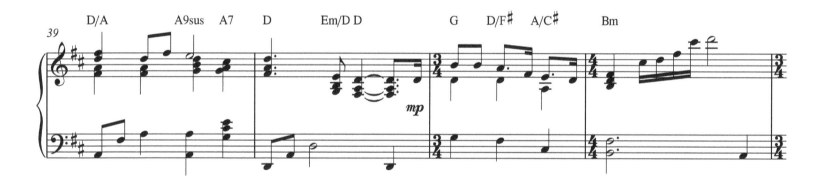

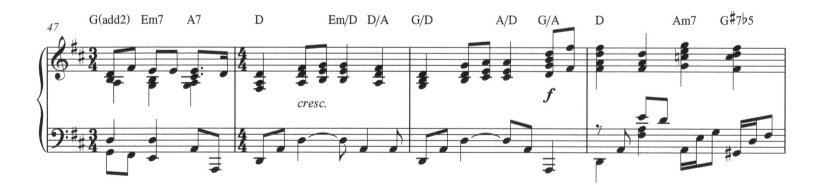

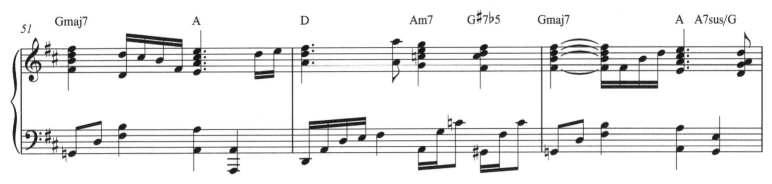

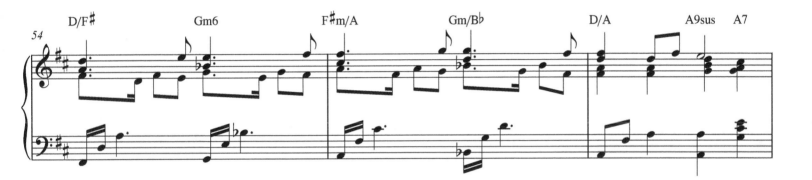

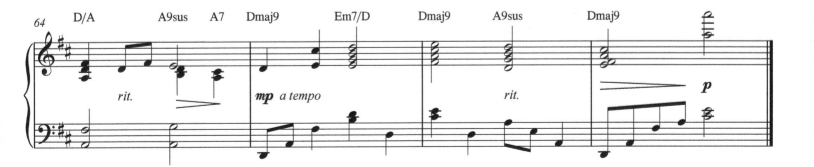

OPEN THE EYES OF MY HEART

Words and Music by
PAUL BALOCHE
Arranged by Mark Hayes

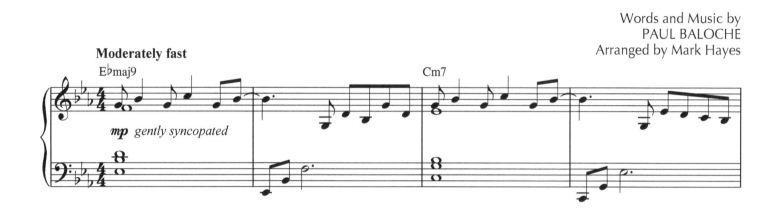

Duration: 2:45

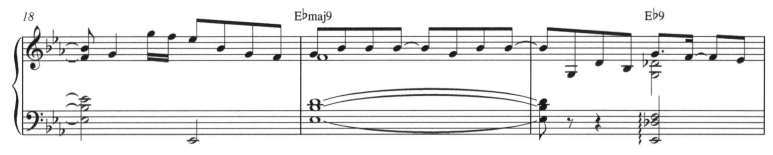

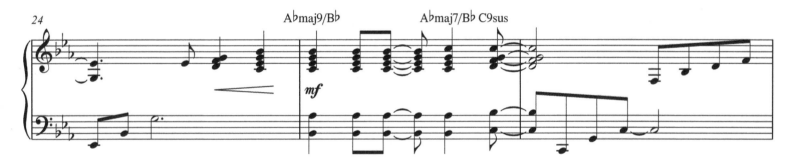

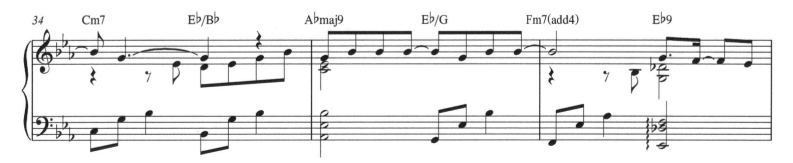

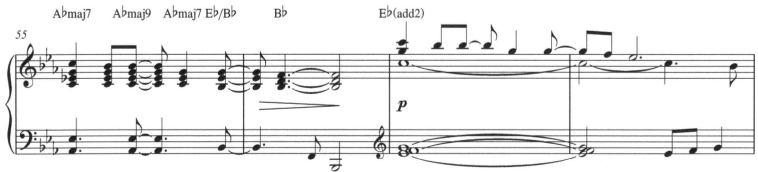

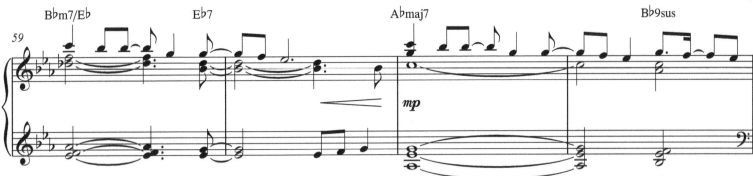

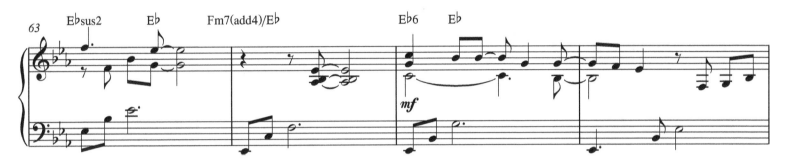

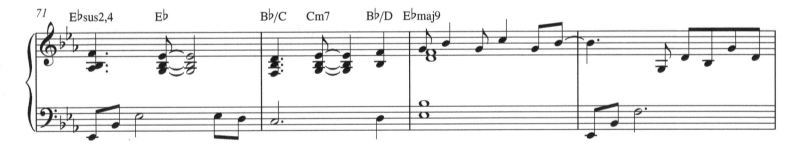

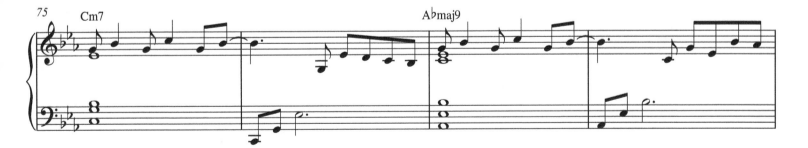

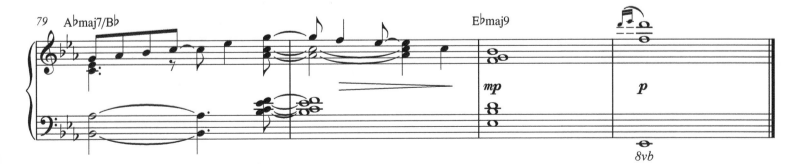

10,000 REASONS
(Bless the Lord)

Words and Music by JONAS MYRIN
and MATT REDMAN
Arranged by Mark Hayes

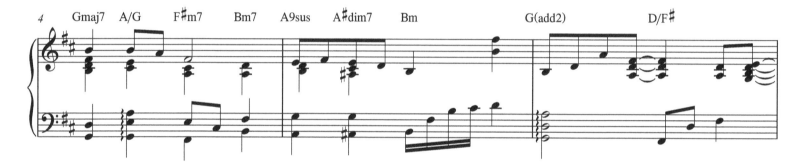

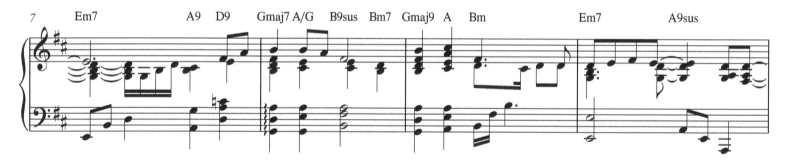

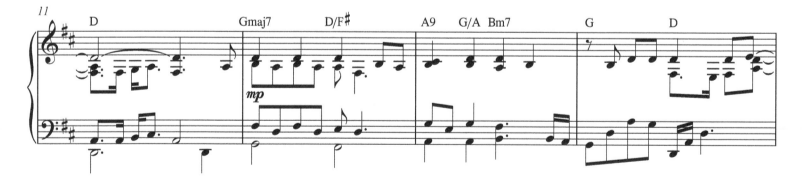

Duration: 3:10

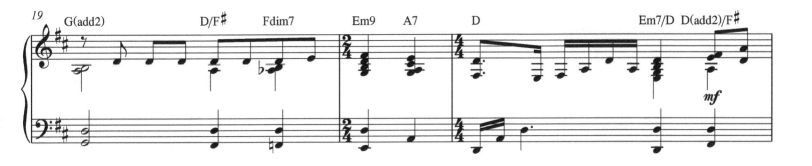

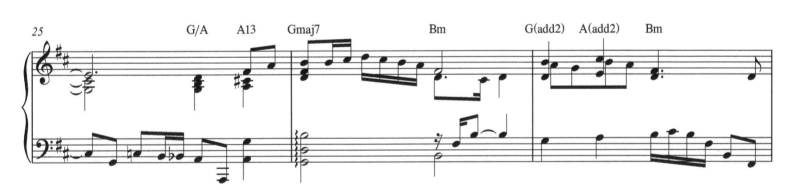

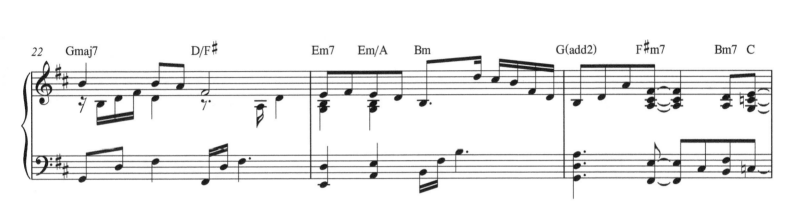

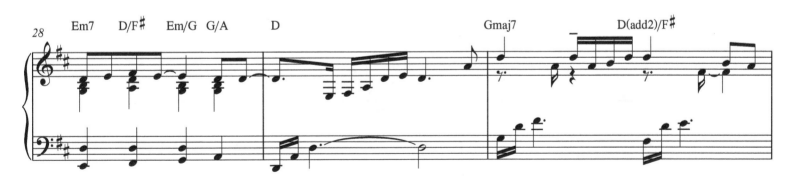

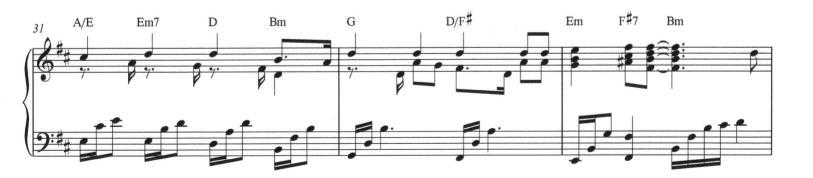

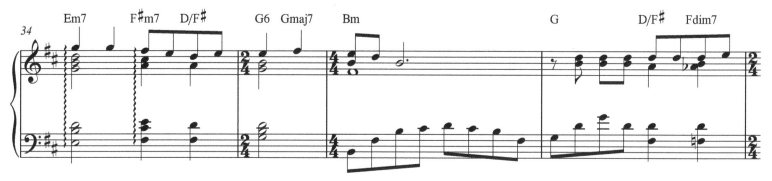

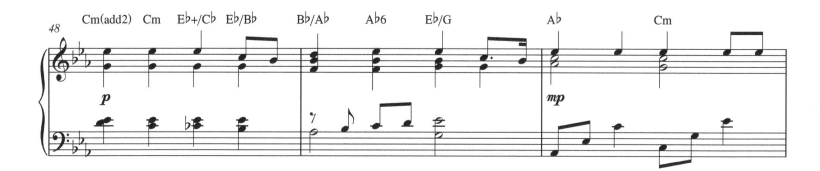

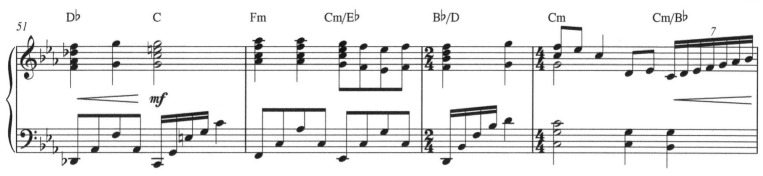

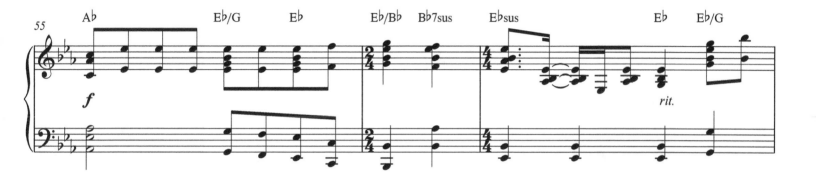

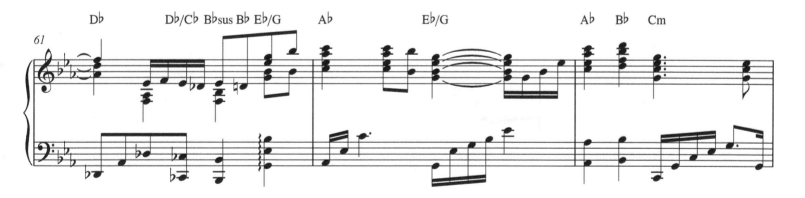

YET NOT I
BUT THROUGH CHRIST IN ME

Words and Music by MICHAEL FARREN,
JONNY ROBINSON and RICH THOMPSON
Arranged by Mark Hayes

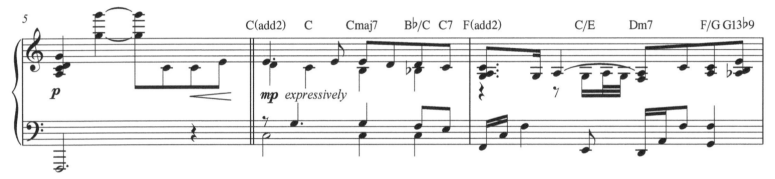

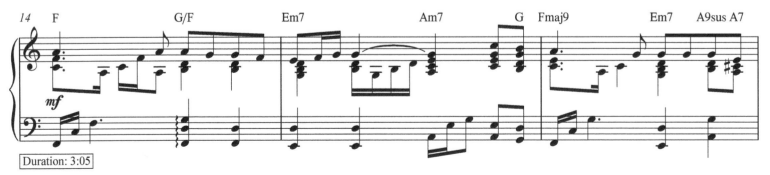

Duration: 3:05

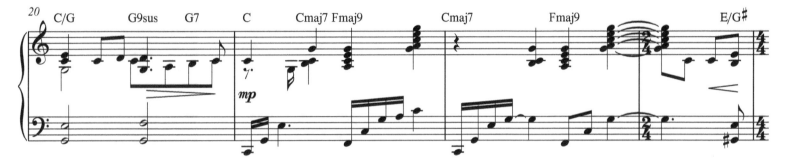

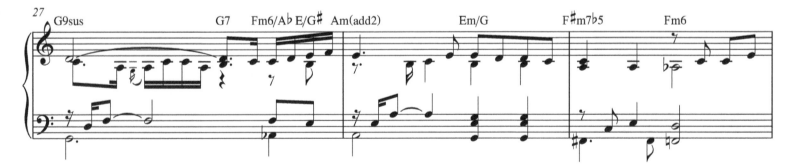

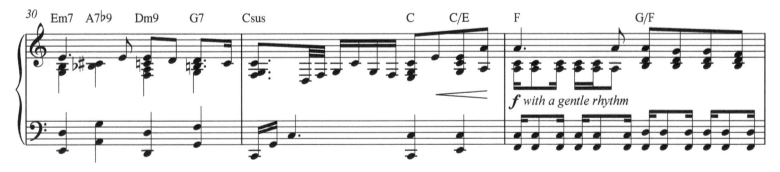

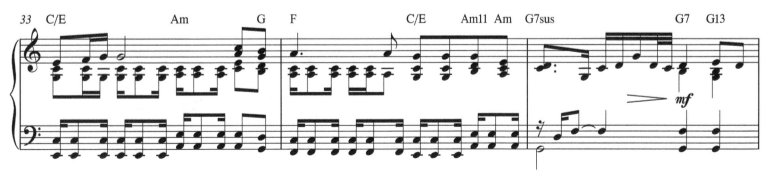

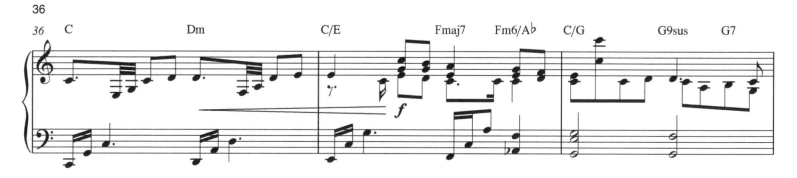

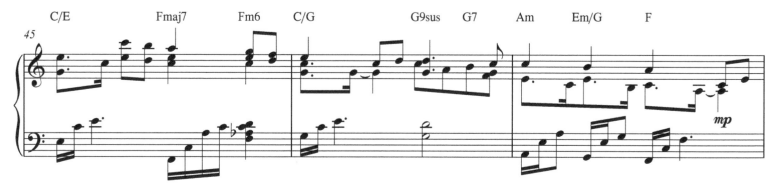

YOUR NAME

Words and Music by PAUL BALOCHE
and GLENN PACKIAM
Arranged by Mark Hayes

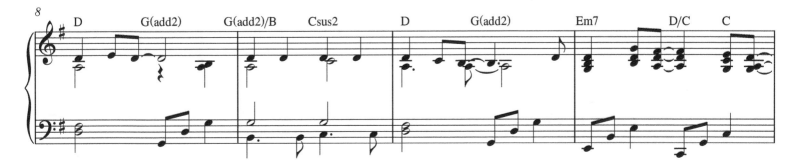

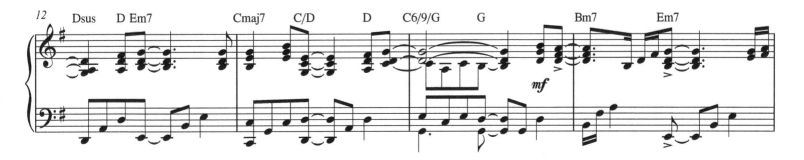

Duration: 3:00

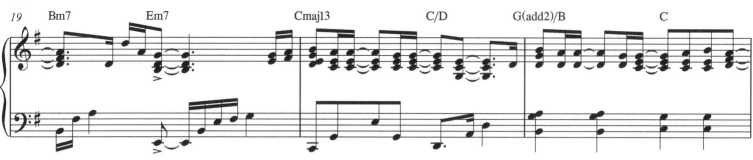

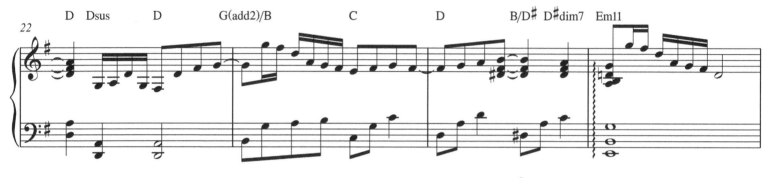

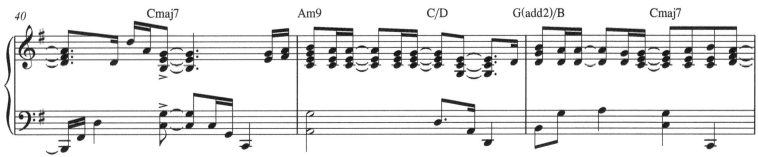

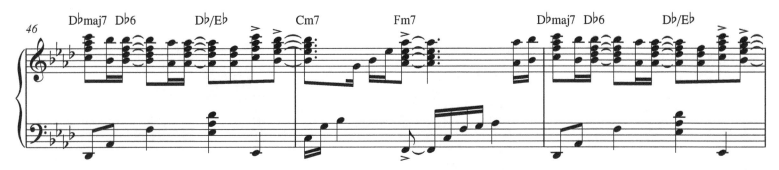

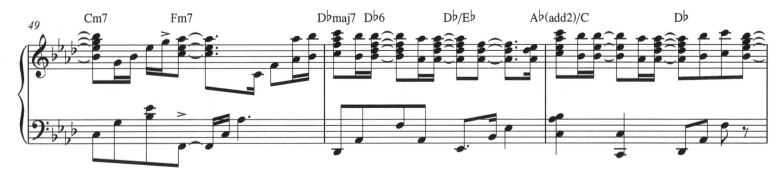

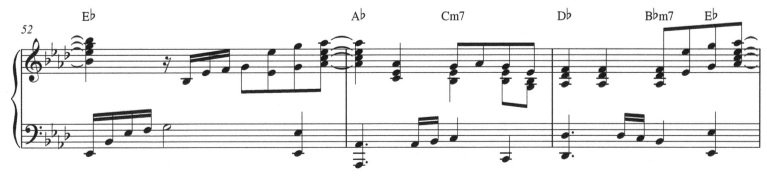

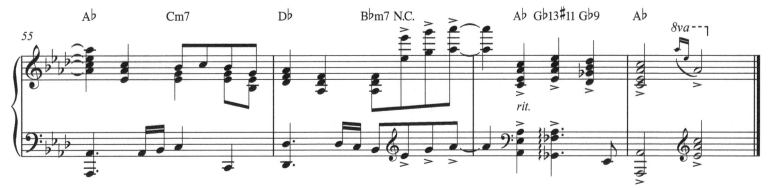

MORE GREAT SONGBOOKS FROM MARK HAYES

Mark Hayes is an award-winning concert pianist, composer and arranger of choral, piano and orchestral music, with over 1500 published works to his credit.

CONTEMPORARY WORSHIP CLASSICS
Hal Leonard

These ten intermediate piano solos, infused with rich harmonic language and hints of jazz, will be welcome in both church and home: Amazing Grace (My Chains Are Gone) • Cornerstone • How Deep the Father's Love for Us • In Christ Alone • Living Hope • Lord, I Need You • Open the Eyes of My Heart • 10,000 Reasons (Bless the Lord) • Yet Not I But Through Christ in Me • Your Name

00385387 .... $14.99

FILM FAVORITES
Hal Leonard

Ten tunes from Tinseltown masterfully arranged by Mark Hayes for piano solo. Includes: Climb Ev'ry Mountain (from The Sound of Music) • Gabriel's Oboe (from The Mission) • God Help the Outcasts (from The Hunchback of Notre Dame) • If I Only Had a Brain (from The Wizard of Oz) • Part of Your World (from The Little Mermaid) • People (from Funny Girl) • Theme from Schindler's List • Singin' in the Rain • Somewhere, My Love (from Doctor Zhivago) • Unchained Melody.

0033449 .... $14.99

THE BEST OF MARK HAYES
Shawnee Press

Includes: Tribute to America • Savior, Like a Shepherd Lead Us • His Eye Is On the Sparrow • Amazing Grace • It Is Well with My Soul • and many more.

35022779 Piano Solo $24.99

THE BEST OF MARK HAYES – VOLUME 2
Shawnee Press

This stellar second volume focuses on contemporary classics arranged with that unmistakable Mark Hayes touch. An essential and permanent addition to your keyboard library! Includes: Great Is Thy Faithfulness • People Need the Lord • and more.

35022781 Piano Solo $24.99

MARK HAYES SELECTS – VOLUME 1
Fred Bock Music Company

This collection includes ten of his best arrangements for piano solo: All Creatures of Our God and King • Beneath the Cross of Jesus • Christ the Lord Is Risen Today • For the Beauty of the Earth • Let All Things Now Living • and more.

08752112 Piano Solo $19.99

HOLY, HOLY, HOLY
Shawnee Press

9 songs arranged for piano and organ duet, including: Fairest Lord Jesus • Holy Holy Holy • In the Garden • O Sacred Head, Now Wounded • and more. 2 books provided, one for each player.

35009567 .... $42.99

WELL-TEMPERED CHRISTMAS
Shawnee Press

This collection contains something for everyone ... a bluesy spiritual, gentle lullabies, concert pieces, lush settings of old favorites and even a medley of secular titles. Mark Hayes' style is unlike any other. Some easy, some not so easy, but all are exciting. Songs include: We Three Kings • I Wonder as I Wander • Rise Up Shepherd and Follow • O Little Town of Bethlehem • Masters in this Hall • Manger Medley • and four more. Highly recommended!

35025350 Piano Solo (Book Only) $19.99

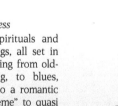

WELL-TEMPERED JAZZ
Shawnee Press

Favorite spirituals and gospel songs, all set in styles ranging from old-time swing, to blues, to bossa, to a romantic "movie theme" to quasi new age stylings. Songs include: Amazing Grace • Every Time I Feel the Spirit • Just a Closer Walk with Thee • Old Time Religion/Swing Low, Sweet Chariot • and more.

35025356 Solo Piano Book $19.99

WELL-TEMPERED PRAISE 1
Shawnee Press

Mark's very first published piano collection, this book is for the advanced pianist and is ideal for preludes, offertories, or the concert stage. "It Is Well with My Soul" is a definite stand-out!

35025364 Piano Solo $19.99

WELL-TEMPERED PRAISE 2
Shawnee Press

This volume continues the classical piano feel of Well-Tempered Praise with tremendous concert arrangements of famous hymn tunes and "get down" versions of beloved gospel songs. Seasonal selections for Christmas and Easter round out this collection. Includes: Praise to the Lord, the Almighty • Higher Ground • Alfred Burt Carol Medley • How Majestic Is Your Name • and more.

35025370 Piano Solo $19.99

WELL-TEMPERED PRAISE 3
Shawnee Press

Audiences will thrill to the jazz sounds of "Joshua Fit the Battle of Jericho" and the romantic, classical quality of "I Need Thee Every Hour." For the advanced pianist, Vol. III in the Well-Tempered Praise series is perfect for use in all kinds of worship settings, recitals, and concerts. It contains a well-chosen mix of hymns, spirituals, and contemporary Christian songs, as well as an original composition by Mark Hayes entitled, "Joysong."

35025375 Piano Solo $19.99

HAL•LEONARD®

www.halleonard.com

Prices, contents, and availability subject to change without notice.

Visit our website for full song lists.